B.L.U.E. PRINT TO YOUR BEST RETIREMENT

How to Access Your Retirement Account Penalty and Tax-Free

DANIEL BLUE

Edited by Hilary Jastram

EARLY PRAISE FOR
B.L.U.E. PRINT TO YOUR BEST RETIREMENT

"As an entrepreneur who came from a prestigious corp career, I felt embarrassed by not having a great knowledge about retirement and creating lasting wealth. Daniel was able to not only take care of my money but explain it to me in a way where I felt smarter and more empowered for the future. Every ounce of knowledge he shares is such gold, and I'm so grateful to have his advice to guide me on my financial literacy journey. His passion about wealth and making people feel secure about their finances is unsurpassed. Take his advice step by step and start to see how your confidence in your financial freedom grows!"

—Shannel Rivera,
CEO, and Founder of Beauty and Hustle

"Daniel Blue is a smart, ethical, and hard-working dude who I'm grateful to be friends with. He works hard in every aspect of his life, and his success in business is no surprise. He's a father, husband, leader, and friend that many people look up to."

—Adam Niec,
CEO of Certain Pay

"When it comes to retirement accounts, no one is better than Daniel Blue. I co-own an accounting firm, and we've referred countless customers to him. Accounting firms are big targets for those in the financial space. They want to partner with accounting firms to get access to our customers to offer their services. We've turned down handfuls of people/companies. Anytime you refer a customer to another company, you're putting your name on the line, so we ALWAYS said no, until we met Daniel. He operates with the best intentions for the person, not his business. He always keeps what's best for the customers top of mind. We've only received positive feedback from our referrals. He makes us look good by honoring what's best for the customers versus what's best for his bottom dollar. Daniel is the only person I've met in the financial world that is a trusted source for unbiased retirement information. Unbiased information is accurate information."

—Trevor Cowley,
Host of the top 1% podcast: *Real Business Owners*

"There are few professionals that I trust with the level of certainty that I have for Daniel Blue. His knowledge of how to take your hard-earned dollars and turn them into a vehicle to accomplish your dreams is second to none. What most impresses me is Dan's level of integrity in an industry that's known for always paying the 'house' and leaving customers' goals as a second thought. I am grateful that Dan chose to write a book that truly shows how an everyday person can finally have their money work for them, instead of the other way around. I cannot recommend this book highly enough."

—Kris Whitehead,
CEO/Founder of Iconic Alliance and NECR, LLC

"Daniel Blue has turned out to be more than just a business acquaintance; he's become a dear friend. His knowledge and expertise are just the beginning of why we've referred so many of our own customers to him over the last five years. Now, he's a very valuable part of our network, and this book he has created is full of value which comes as no surprise considering he is a person of value."

—Kale Goodman,
Co-founder, Easier Accounting

"My favorite part about Daniel Blue, aside from his authenticity and his work ethic, is his ability to simplify the complicated parts of creating long-term wealth. Daniel always goes above and beyond to make sure his customers feel like family and know that he always has their best interests at heart. It's an honor to watch and be part of his incredible journey from rock bottom to the most elite version of himself."

—Drewbie Wilson,
Vice President of Break Free Academy

RESOURCES

DANIELBLUE.ME

DEDICATION

For my mom, the person who taught me to keep taking action and not complain, no matter how hard the challenge is.

TABLE OF CONTENTS

FOREWORD

The fact that you're reading this book means you're interested in your future.

My name is Ryan Stewman, and I believe that people don't necessarily need to retire. They need to build passive streams of income and own their funds. Most of us entrepreneurs and financially savvy people don't want to retire anyway. We don't want to work as hard as we might be working now forever. But we've also seen too many people retire and let themselves go. We've even seen them pass away or spend 10 years out of the workforce, only to have to search for a job when they run low on money.

Retirement's not the answer. The answer is owning assets that create passive income. And that's actually how I met Daniel Blue, the author of this book.

Daniel operates his business to keep you in the know. He is aware of what most people don't know when it comes to their retirement accounts. He also has the full scoop of what the media, the big banks, the giant hedge funds, and the 401(k) companies try to keep you from learning because it would hurt their business. When you learn what he is sharing within these pages, you will ask the questions: *why would you pay the big banks, the big brokers, or any other big money name to do what you can simply do for yourself? Don't you want to have more control over your money and fewer fees, to generate more income?* Of course, you do.

Let's say that you spend a million dollars a year on your investment portfolio. The bank will charge you $50,000 a year to manage your money. They charge this to allocate your money, draw up contracts, and perform every other duty necessary to take care of your accounts. You will get this bill every year.

Now, what if you took that same $50,000 and invested it at just 10% year over year? You would double your money in a short period of time. You would pay your newly reallocated money to the bank and will have accomplished managing your money yourself. People think that to handle their money they must be super educated, but you don't even need to be that financially savvy. You don't have to be intimidated by what you don't know.

I used Daniel's program, sold some stocks, then took money out of my E-Trade account to test what he had been educating me on. I put my money into an account that he suggested and because I took his advice, I was able to purchase 10 restaurants. Those restaurants produce cash flow every single month. That cash flow surpasses any equity I could have gained by simply owning stocks, but I never knew this. I would have kept doing the same old thing, throwing my money away, if I hadn't met Daniel.

As you'll learn in this book, when you can manage your money and be smart about it, you can set yourself up to win in the end. And I don't just mean in retirement. I mean you can live the rest of your life as the best of your life through passive income.

This knowledge and this book are the missing pieces to your financial puzzle that you have been looking for. Daniel is an amazing person and you're going to love what you're about to read. Apply it and you can change the course of your life.

Ryan Stewman
Founder of Apex

INTRODUCTION

Have you ever learned something financially important and asked yourself "Why wasn't I taught this in school?"

Unfortunately, our schools, most financial advisers, and CPAs don't teach us some of the financial strategies that could most alter our lifestyles for the better.

I wrote this book to break down basic terms and financial concepts about retirement accounts. I know, I know, the phrase "retirement accounts" sounds boring; however, this book will not put you to sleep.

In fact, it will help you sleep better at night, knowing you will have a brighter financial future where you can worry less and have more money in your pocket.

Each chapter covers ways to make money tax-free, pay off debt, invest outside the stock market with your IRA/401(k), get funding for your business without the banks, and much more. Feel free to hop around from chapter to chapter depending on your financial needs.

The acronym B.L.U.E in the title of this book, "B.L.U.E Print To Your Best Retirement," stands for:

Build
Learn
Utilize
Enjoy

I want to help you build, learn, utilize and enjoy your money in ways that give you happiness.

Money doesn't buy happiness, but whatever your goals are in life, more money can most likely help you accomplish them.

At the end of the book, I am offering you the opportunity to take a financial course called "How to Make Money Tax-free." This course will help you make more money. It's easy to follow along, short and straight to the point – just the thing to put you on the right financial track for your foreseeable future.

Enjoy the book, and your new peace of mind.

CHAPTER 1: INTRODUCTION TO 401(K)/IRAS

*"Do not save what is left after spending,
but spend what is left after saving."*
—*Warren Buffett*

What's the first thing that comes to your mind when you think about retirement?

Most people think of Social Security and some type of pension. But did you know that Social Security is only designed to replace around 40% of the average American's worker's income?

As far as pensions go, those are few and far between. Very few companies even offer pensions anymore.

It was the disappearing pension that prompted the government to introduce the Traditional Individual Retirement Account (IRA) in 1974.

The Traditional IRA was defined as a retirement vehicle to supplement pensions and Social Security and is the most popular IRA available.

But what does all of this mean for you?

If Social Security is designed to replace only around 40% of our income, what happens when our income drops but our expenses don't?

Consider also that no one knows the future. All it takes is one health disaster for you or someone in your family to set you back financially. Medical insurance and expenses are constantly on the rise. It's not unheard of for people in their sixties to be paying close to $1,000 in monthly premiums for their health insurance. This is just one reason why we have to make a plan for our future before it's too late.

Of course, people don't plan on failing financially when they are retired. They don't plan on living on a fixed income, either – but if they fail to plan properly, the last few chapters of their life can be painful financially.

This begs the question: how can we avoid experiencing pain financially when we get older?

If you are reading this, you most likely are self-employed. The good news is that being self-employed gives you access to unique retirement accounts that can prepare you to live a better life financially as you get older. The problem is that no one has likely talked to you about this. You will find out why as you get deeper into this book.

To make this as easy as possible, let me compare retirement accounts to something we all understand: vehicles and gas.

The retirement vehicle is, for example, the IRA or the 401(k). The gas is whatever makes the retirement vehicle go forward (making money), or backward (losing money). Let's say your 401(k) holds mutual funds. In this case the vehicle is the 401(k) and the gas is the mutual fund.

Before we can go any further, we need to know what the difference is between the different retirement vehicles.

IRA

An IRA is one type of retirement vehicle. Anyone with a Social Security number and earned income can set up an IRA. Folks who don't have access to a 401(k) through their job or would like to have more saving options put money into their IRA. As of the first quarter in 2021, assets in IRAs totaled 12.6 trillion.[1]

There are a few different components to an IRA that you should be aware of.

1. The most that you can contribute into an IRA as of 2021 is $6,000 per year if you are under the age of fifty.

2. Once you are over the age of 50, you can contribute up to $7,000 a year.

---

[1] "Release: Quarterly Retirement Market Data, First Quarter 2021." Investment Company Institute, June 16, 2021. https://www.ici.org/statistical-report/ret_21_q1.

There are also some tax benefits when you put money into an IRA that you should be aware of.

1. With a traditional IRA, the money you invest is tax-deductible. So if you make $50,000 one year, and you put $5,000 into your traditional IRA, you're going to get a $5,000 write-off against your income that same year. This means instead of paying taxes on $50,000 in income that year, you will pay taxes on $45,000. That's an immediate tax write-off.

2. That money is then identified as what's called "tax-deferred" while it is growing in your account. However, once you take the money out, you will have to pay taxes on that money.

ROTH IRA

A Roth IRA, on the other hand, is the exact opposite.

1. When you invest money into a Roth IRA, you will have to pay taxes on that amount that same year. You do not get the tax benefit upfront.

2. But . . . that money then grows in your account tax-FREE. Meaning that if you put $5,000 into your Roth IRA, and it grows to $10,000, the full balance of your account is tax-free.

3. In general, you can withdraw your earnings without owning taxes or penalties if you are at least 59 ½ years old and it's been at least five years since you first contributed money into any Roth IRA.

Both the traditional IRA and the Roth IRA were designed to encourage people to save money for retirement. The tax benefits were added as an incentive for the people who took advantage of the account and invested their money.

TRADITIONAL SAVINGS ACCOUNT

Conversely, if you put money into a traditional savings account, there are really no tax benefits. But doing this does give you peace of mind, knowing your cash is readily available in your savings account.

And while this is an option to save money, you want to be careful not to have too much money in savings as that money isn't earning you much interest either.

It's a good idea to have some liquid cash in savings in case of an emergency, but why not take advantage of putting your cash into an account that grows faster than a savings account and gives you tax savings?

BUT I CAN'T ACCESS *MY MONEY*

Some people are afraid of putting money into a retirement account because they feel they won't be able to touch their money until retirement age. That's not always the case, as you will find out as you continue reading this book.

Here is an illustration showing the difference between having your money invested in a Roth IRA versus having it in a taxable account (i.e., holding your money outside a retirement vehicle).

As you can see, there is a huge difference in dollars when you have your money invested inside a retirement account versus having it invested in a taxable account.

The problem is that most people's associations with IRA/401(k)s are that they tie up your money and you can never touch it. That is a myth that I will cover in more detail later in this book.

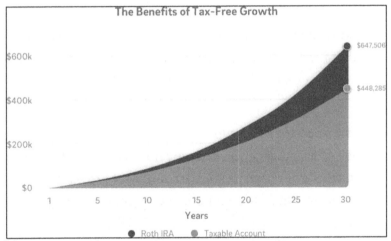

Assumptions: This chart is for illustrative purposes and does not represent an actual investment. It assumes a 7.8% annual return in each account over the 30 years. The annual investment growth in the taxable account is taxed 25% at the end of each year and the Roth IRA is never taxed.[2]

---

[2] Chart source: https://www.brightplan.com/blog/5-reasons-to-open-an-ira-and-max-it-out-every-year

FLEXIBILITY

An IRA does have a fundamental issue: a lack of flexibility. People make a valid point when they say things like "IRAs are terrible. I can't even control my own money. I won't even be able to touch my own money until I am retired!"

Yes, you can't tap into the IRA, for the most part, without paying a 10% early withdrawal penalty to the IRS. However, there are a couple of exceptions.

You can avoid paying penalties and taxes on IRA withdrawals, as long as you put the money back within 60 days.

There are also 9 penalty-free withdrawals that can be made from an IRA. These include: unreimbursed medicals expenses; health insurance premiums while unemployed; permanent disability; higher education expenses; you inherit an IRA; you buy a home as a first-time homeowner; substantially equal periodic payments; to fulfill an IRS levy; and being called to active duty.[3]

If you ever try to withdraw money from a traditional IRA, you will have to pay a 10% early withdrawal penalty if you're under 59 ½, and you will have to pay taxes on that money as well as claim your withdrawal as taxable income. Doing this

---

[3] Folger, Jean. "9 Penalty-Free IRA Withdrawals." Investopedia. Investopedia, May 19, 2021.
https://www.investopedia.com/articles/retirement/02/111202.asp.

has really bitten people in the butt. That's money they could have used when they got older and retired.

MY CONSTRUCTION CUSTOMER

I was talking to a customer not long ago and learned they had yanked out $50,000 from their IRA. They needed the money for their construction business, but because they were under 59 ½, they got hit with a 10% early withdrawal penalty. That's a quick $5,000 that went right to the IRS. Plus, they had to claim their $50,000 withdrawal as income, so they were taxed at about 20-25%. Let's do the math: the $50,000 that they took out ended up costing around $15,000 in penalties and taxes, meaning that $50,000 really ended up being only $30,000-$35,000 after all the penalties and taxes to the IRS.

When you're in a situation like that, you have to ask yourself whether it's really worth it — or if there is another way to resolve what you need.

This is part of the reason I think it is so important for people to really understand the different vehicles that are out there. And with the IRA being the most popular, other than a 401(k) through an employer, you need to know it can definitely serve its purpose and be useful and beneficial.

That said, make sure you know what you're getting yourself into and that you understand what the IRA can and can't do. That way you really have a full understanding when it comes to your dollars.

IRA BANKRUPTCY PROTECTION

It's also important to know money in an IRA is protected from bankruptcy. No one wants to file for bankruptcy, but in most cases, if you do file for bankruptcy, your IRA dollars won't be lost. If you ever had to file bankruptcy, your traditional or Roth IRA would be protected to a total value of 1,362,800 as of 2019.[4]

Here's a recap of the difference between a traditional IRA and a Roth IRA:

TRADITIONAL IRA

- $6-$7k annual contribution limit

- Contributions give you a tax write-off that year

- Money grows tax-deferred. You pay taxes on that money when you pull it out

ROTH IRA

- $6-$7k annual contribution limit

- You pay taxes on the contributions you make into the account that year

- Money grows tax-free

---

[4] Carpenter, J. William. "Is My IRA Protected in a Bankruptcy?" Investopedia. Investopedia, May 19, 2021. https://www.investopedia.com /ask/answers/081915/my-ira-protected-bankruptcy.asp.

- If you are over 59 ½ years of age and your account is at least five years old, you can withdraw contributions and earnings with no tax or penalty

- You can always withdraw the money you contributed with no tax or penalty

If you are an entrepreneur, you will learn in the next chapter that the IRS will give you certain financial advantages in the retirement account arena as compared to people who aren't in business for themselves.

That's information you will want to pay attention to!

For more valuable information that will last you a lifetime of earning, please sign up for my course "The Quest Way – How to Grow Your Money Tax Free" at

BluePrintRetirementCourse.com

You'll get the reader-exclusive price of $47, compared to the regular price of $297. Just visit the link above and register! It's that easy.

CHAPTER 2: ENTREPRENEURS GET ACCESS TO BETTER RETIREMENT ACCOUNTS

*"Guess who votes on bills that are related to
retirement accounts? Congress. Guess which group
consists of a lot of business owners? Congress."*
—Daniel Blue

Most people can agree that American business owners are treated differently when it comes to their finances. They get a lot more advantages, for example. We know that people like Jeff Bezos and Warren Buffet get multiple tax breaks, loopholes, and advantages that the average W2 employee doesn't… For instance, did you know that Warren Buffet is on record as saying that he pays a lower tax rate than his secretary? That's because he's an entrepreneur. It's proof that business owners get more tax advantages than the average 9-5, W2 employee.

Business owners in America are in an advantageous position. They can get more dollars in their pockets, accrue more savings and benefits, and can use more exceptions, especially when it comes to processing their taxes. They get certain tax write-offs and credits that aren't available to non-business owners.

For ease of explanation, I will split taxes into two categories, individual and business. I've found that doing this makes what I am sharing with you in this book easier to understand.

We can split up retirement accounts in the same way. There are retirement accounts for individuals, and retirement accounts for business owners.

To properly lay down the foundation of these differences we are going to dive into, let's start with examining the pros and cons of these retirement options:

RETIREMENT ACCOUNTS FOR INDIVIDUALS

The most popular retirement accounts for individuals are 401(k)s where a W2 employee can contribute through an employer.

Another popular retirement account for individuals is an IRA. IRA stands for "Individual Retirement Account."

Both of these accounts have a lot of limitations.

As of 2021, the IRS states you can only contribute $6,000-7,000 dollars per year of new money to an IRA. So, let's do the math again: if you're trying to save hundreds of thousands of dollars but are only able to only put $6,000-7,000 dollars per year into this plan, this is not super beneficial for you.

Combine that with the fact that, as I shared, if you take money out an IRA, you can't do it without getting penalized by the IRA *and* the IRS. That penalty can be 10% of what you can take out, and it can even be up to 30-35% of what you take out after you pay penalties and taxes (depending on your tax bracket, too).

Ouch. That's a lot of money to lose.

THE REAL ESTATE DEAL

I once spoke with a lady who wanted to invest $100,000 into a real estate deal from her IRA. She went to her financial adviser to get help on how to facilitate this. The response that she got from her financial adviser led her to withdraw the $100,000 and take a tax and penalty hit that cost her $30,000. If only she had known there was a way to invest that same $100,000 into that same real estate deal and not have to pay the $30,000 tax penalty.

I talked to her about some of the strategies I'm sharing with you in this book. She replied that if I had talked to her before she had taken out that $100,000 for her real estate deal, I would have saved her $30,000.

You might remember the day when you signed up for a 401(k) through your job. You were making W2 wages and putting money into a 401(k). You met with the benefits representative who walked you through a handful of options to choose from. You filled out some paperwork as you asked yourself, *do I want a conservative approach*? *Do I want a moderate approach or an aggressive approach?* Aside from your mind spinning, there's not a lot of thought that goes into how 401(k) employee accounts work. You were likely shown a basic menu of different mutual funds that you could work with.

But have you ever thought about who put together that menu? You know it's not you; it might surprise you to hear that it's not your employer, either.

As of 2021, if you are an employee, you can contribute up to $19,500 per year into a 401(k). An additional $6,500 can be contributed for workers over 50 years of age.

Your employer's going to use a company like Fidelity or Vanguard to hold your 401(k) dollars. That company will give your representative a pre-selected menu they allow you to choose from.

As the employee, you can circle a few of those options and put your money in. You literally get minutes to decide how prosperous or not your future will be.

If you think about it this way, you don't really call the shots in this plan. You don't really call the shots in this massive chunk of your life.

Would you be so complacent as to allow someone else to pick where you work or how much money you would accept for your salary? Of course not!

Both of these decisions determine your income and your lifestyle. But most people just blindly do what they are told and trust their employer to deliver an extremely simplified menu.

But let's get out of that headspace for a minute and change the topic to what you can accomplish as an entrepreneur.

RETIREMENT ACCOUNTS FOR AN ENTREPRENEUR

If you open a retirement account as a business owner, the IRS essentially says to you, "If you're a business owner with 1099 income, owning a sole proprietorship, LLC, an S Corp, or you're a C-corp, we will allow you to set up your retirement *these two* ways: you get to choose from a SEP IRA and SIMPLE IRA."

Although their names sound fancy, these are just good old-fashioned IRAs, but they do have higher contribution limits. A SEP IRA allows up to 25% of employee compensation, with the max being $58,000 as of the year 2021. The SIMPLE IRA maximum annual contribution is $13,500.

If you are a solopreneur, you can also choose to use a Solo 401(k). Maybe you are a real estate agent that gets 1099 commission, or you are a freelancer, consultant, or other type of business owner who doesn't have W2 employees except for you or your spouse. This retirement plan is not talked about much because more people are aware of SEP IRAs and SIMPLE IRAs that Solo 401(k)s. In my opinion, IRAs are talked about more than Solo 401(k)s because Wall Street wants to charge you fees and they don't want you to take your retirement money out.

If you are a business owner with high interest rate debt you're trying to pay off, a Solo 401(k) can provide you a way to pay off that debt. The main problem it can solve is helping people access their retirement account dollars penalty- and tax-free before retirement age. It also gives you more investment options aside from just the stock market.

I don't want to overwhelm you, so I will take the next couple of chapters to explain more of the facts that you will find helpful.

My goal is to show you how to use these accounts to your advantage. I want to help you start accomplishing some of your business and financial goals immediately — not when you are 70 years old and just retired from your 9-5 job.

For more valuable information that will last you a lifetime of earning, please sign up for my course "The Quest Way – How to Grow Your Money Tax Free" at

BluePrintRetirementCourse.com

You'll get the reader-exclusive price of $47, compared to the regular price of $297. Just visit the link above and register! It's that easy.

CHAPTER 3: DO 401(K)S SUCK?

"Ignorance breeds fear."
—*Mike Wilson*

Over the years, my customer's feedback on 401(k) retirement accounts has been terrible.

You name it, I've heard it – most popularly that…

- "401(k) is a scam."
- "I don't have a lot of options."
- "It's not growing a lot."
- "I don't have any control over it."
- "It's locked up."
- "I don't know how to get to it."
- "The statements are complicated to read."
- "I don't know how much is in there, so how can I prepare for my future?"
- "If I decide I don't want the account anymore, I can't get all my money back and have to pay a penalty. That's not fair!"
- "I'm giving them money and they're not telling me anything."
- "All I hear is 'blue chip stock.' Where is it going?"

Throughout my career, I've learned that there are a few reasons why people are complaining about 401(k)s. Here are some of the more common complaints.

SUPER-HIGH EXPECTATIONS

Usually, the people complaining about their 401(k)s have established them through their current employer.

For example, they might be working at UPS. In our scenario, when they first started working for UPS, they sat down and filled out some paperwork to get their 401(k) set up. At the time they were probably under the illusion that the 401(k) would be some awesome savings vehicle. They were excited because they'd get a good employer match, and so they assumed they could save a bunch of money. That means they entered into the agreement with super-high expectations, so after a bit, and learning the truth, they would feel let down.

Employer 401(k)s are a little like a bait and switch. The employee thought they were buying into one thing, only to learn it was something completely different. They actually can't control their own money. They don't have much flexibility or options with the 401(k). A big complaint of many people is that they can't touch it without a penalty.

If you're in this boat, let's go back in time to the first day you enrolled in your 401(k). As we discussed earlier, you signed some paperwork that allowed you to choose if you wanted conservative, aggressive, or moderate investment options. You filled in a couple of bubbles, circled a few options, signed your name, and next thing you knew, money was getting deducted from your paycheck and going into your 401(k). After studying your paystub, you probably noticed you were getting a match from your employer. Typically, they give you a 3% or 6% match. Finally, your money was invested in the stock market. Regardless of what plan you chose, you were still limited to the options your employer gave you.

Understand, in the case of our employee at UPS, that UPS doesn't hold their money. UPS uses a financial company like Fidelity, Vanguard, or some other massive firm to actually hold the 401(k).

In the case of UPS's and Fidelity's relationship, before they even met with you, they agreed on certain criteria to set up your 401(k). UPS calls the shots, because they're the employer. They're the ones providing you the options. You're just the participant. You don't get to make up or call the rules in the game. You're a player on the team and you have to do what you're told. That's why people get mad. They learn after they dig into the policy, or maybe they want to move some money around, that, "Shoot, because I don't call the shots, I don't get a lot of options. I don't get a lot of say on what to do with my money even though I earned it and it's mine!" Their anger compounds the more they think about it, then they get stuck in a question loop, *why can't I choose what to do with my money? Why, why do I have to listen to someone else and follow their rules and all these restrictions?* Learning the truth of your limitations is a big, ugly wake-up call.

That's a big disconnect between the expectations of the employer and the reality.

GIMME MY MONEY

As I discussed, if I had an employee 401(k) and wanted to take out $10,000 of my money, but was only given $6,000, I would be livid, too. *I just lost $4,000 to the IRS?* The frustration is understandable.

I CAN'T GROW MY MONEY ANY OTHER WAY?!?

People also don't think it is fair that the money going into a 401(k) can only come from your paycheck through the job where you signed up for it. If you've sold your house or have a side hustle and earn money from that, you can't deposit it into your 401(k). If the account is not through your current employer or job, no dice! That's yet another limitation.

So far, we've uncovered a lot of limits and a lot of grumbling about what you can and can't do with your 401(K).

For example, you can...

1. Invest it in conservative mutual funds.

2. Invest it in aggressive mutual funds.

3. Invest it in moderate mutual funds.

4. *Possibly* benefit from lower fee investments such as index funds or single equities. If you work for Walmart, you might get Walmart shares, while still being limited on where and how you can invest your money as well as how you can withdraw your money.

There are two ways to take money out of a 401(k).

1. As a distribution, which is defined as a withdrawal — so you will be levied the 10% early withdrawal fee if you're under 59½ years old, and you will be levied taxes, which are dependent on your tax bracket. Remember, any withdrawal equals getting nailed by the IRS.

2. As a loan feature. A loan feature works like this. The IRS allows some 401(k) plans where you can take out up to 50% of the account value or $50,000 — whichever number is less. You won't have to pay penalties and taxes on the dollars you take out, because your money is considered a loan. As a loan, you will have to pay back the money within five years to avoid the taxable hit, the penalties, and taxes.

If you opt to do this, then you would have money taken from your paycheck to pay back that loan. Typically, there would be an interest rate on this loan — usually whatever the prime interest rate is plus two points. This could be more or less a range of 5-7%. That interest will generally go back to your 401(k).

Taking a loan out is a great way to access your retirement account dollars without paying the penalties. Maybe you wanted to take some of this money out because you note that your 401(k) is averaging 7-9% a year in interest and you suppose you can take some of that money out and invest it into your business to grow it. Maybe you want to get financing from a bank but need to pay down some credit card debt to raise your credit score. Additionally, your credit card debt might be costing you 20-25% in interest. You can do the math in this scenario: you're making 9% on your money (now designated a loan) versus losing 25% to the bank on the card. It would make sense to pay off a little credit card debt.

If you want to exercise this option, you might find that people say, "Don't do a loan feature on a 401(k). Keep it in the stock market, so it can grow."

Many people have been conditioned to think this way. But there are some instances where it makes sense to take the loan out of your 401(k) so you don't have to pay the penalties and taxes and you can allow your money to work for you in other ways. Or maybe after examining your choices, you don't want to take out that loan. The point is to know that you *do* have choices, and that you can learn about everything you can and can't do and then make an informed decision.

Now, not all 401(k) plans have a loan feature. If you are working for a company that gives you a 401(k) option, you would need to ensure there is language in the plan documentation that states you can take a loan. Sometimes that loan feature is not included in the plan documents. This means that you can't take a loan from your 401(k).

If you are accessing your 401(k) through a previous employer, then you might be quite limited in what you can and can't do. Since you're not working for that company anymore, yet you still have a 401(k) there, you can't contribute any new money into that plan because there's no money that can be taken from your paychecks. You also cannot take advantage of the loan feature. Just make a mental note that if your 401(k) is from your previous employer, you will typically not be able to take a loan from that plan. Of course, this is another reason why 401(k)s leave a lot of people with a bad taste in their mouth.

THE POSITIVES

1. A 401(k) gives you tax benefits. Whether those tax benefits outweigh the limitations is up to you and your financial situation.

2. It allows you to save for the future.

It's always a good idea to research your 401(k) with your employer before you agree to anything. Find out if there is a loan feature on the plan. Learn about the investment options. Understand whether you will get matching contributions. Really peel back the layers to find out what you can and can't do.

MY FORGETFUL CUSTOMER

I was recently talking with someone who had left their job and forgotten about their 401(k) with their previous employer. After several months of statements coming to their door, they took the time to look into the account. That's when they learned the truth about how their investments were performing. As they told me, "I was staring at the statement and saw that geez, I'm not doing that hot with my account. The more I looked into it, the more I discovered that I can't really maneuver my money around. I can't change where my money is invested. I can't add any more to the account, much less draw anything out without paying a penalty." My customer told me that they wanted to pull some of that money out to invest in his business. They had a side business in real estate and were frustrated that they couldn't access any of that money.

Once my customer realized that their 401(k) through their previous employer was super, super limited, they decided to roll the account over to gain more freedom. In a different vehicle, there were a lot more options.

We'll talk about those options in the coming pages.

In the meantime, to get even more information on how to establish and manage your self-retirement accounts, tune in to my podcast: *How Winners Win.*

CHAPTER 4: THE SECRET RETIREMENT ACCOUNT WEAPON

"What the Tesla is to the car industry is what the Solo 401(k) is to the retirement account industry."
—Daniel Blue

In the last chapter, we talked about some of the limitations and complaints surrounding 401(k)s. But what I'd really like to do is help you understand that not all 401(k)s are terrible.

Some 401(k)s can actually benefit you and give you a lot more freedom than you might normally experience.

Obviously, this is not the case with the employer-oriented 401(k)s that we talked about in the previous chapter—whether these accounts are with a current or previous employer. We call an employee version of the 401(k) being handcuffed to the plan.

But what if you're a business owner and you get to call your own shots?

It's true… when you're a business owner, you get to dictate your work schedule. You're not answering to a boss. You have freedom. You get to write off and deduct certain expenses on your taxes.

How nice would it be if you could also get additional benefits through your retirement accounts?

Well, you actually can with the vehicle I introduced earlier — the Solo 401(k)!

THE SOLO 401(K) DEFINED

The simplest definition of the Solo 401(k) is that it is just another version of a 401(k) for the employer — which is to say, you. In this case, to access and use this plan, you can't have any W2 employees aside from you and a spouse. To clarify, 1099 contractors are okay.

Envision that your business has its own LLC. That LLC can have its own retirement account, which would be the Solo 401(k). The Solo 401(k) has a few advantages over a 401(k) utilized through a 9-5 job. Unlike the employer 401(k), where they call the shots, the Solo 401(k) allows YOU call the shots. The only responsibility or obligation you have is to the IRS.

If you have a Solo 401(k) through your business and you aren't contributing any money from your 9-5 job into a 401(k), the max you can contribute into a Solo 401(k) is up to $19,500 as an "employee" of your business. An additional $6,500 can be added into the Solo 401(k) if you are over the age of 50 years old. You can also contribute an additional dollar amount on the "employer" side. In total, you can contribute up to 25% of your W2 wage that you collect from your business.

SAM'S STORY

Sam is 51 years old. He earned $50,000 in W2 wages from his business in 2020. He put $19,500 into his Solo 401(k) on the "employee" side and an extra $6,500 in catch-up contributions since he is over 50 years old.

His business contributed 25% of his W2 compensation to the plan. We know that 25% of $50,000 is $12,500. When you combine the $26,000 that Sam put in on the "employee" side with the $12,500 contributed on the "employer" side, the total dollar amount that Sam contributed to his Solo 401(K) in 2020 was $38,500.

The thrilling aspect of this kind of account is that you can max it out and put up to $58,000 (and additional $6,500 if you are over 50 years old) into the account per year. Because the Solo 401(k) allows you to contribute money into the plan on the "employer" side, the contributions that can be made to a Solo 401(k) are much higher than what can be put into a 401(k) that you would get from a corporate job.

Another nice part about a Solo 401(k) is that you can add your spouse to the plan. Then they will get their own bucket of money.

Assuming the numbers work out for you and your spouse, they could ALSO contribute up to $58,000 per year into the plan. Add those two numbers from you and your spouse together, and we start talking about real money making a real difference in your life.

Combined, you can both contribute up to $116,000 per year with an additional $6,500 each for whoever is over 50 years of age.

Understandably, this gives you tons of tax benefits.

You can choose to make that contribution pre-tax or post-tax, in the case of a Roth account. I will explain how Roth accounts works below. First, let me cover what the process is for a pre-tax contribution.

In a pre-tax contribution, the money that gets put into your Solo 401(k) is 100% tax-deductible that year. If you contributed $58,000 into your Solo 401(k) in 2020, you could then deduct that $58,000 from your income that year — which would give you immediate tax savings. If you do this, however, you are kicking your tax bill down the road, because the $58,000 would grow tax-free inside your Solo 401(k), but when you withdraw the money, you would pay taxes.

GET TAXED ON THE SEED, NOT THE HARVEST

The other type of contribution you can make into your Solo 401(k), and what I touched on above, is called a Roth (post-tax). The funds you contribute into your Roth Solo 401(k) are considered taxable income, so there is no immediate tax break in the year you put the funds into the account. However, the contributions made into the Roth Solo 401(k) grow tax-free AND stay tax-free.

Let's break it down:

- You contribute $25,000 into your Roth Solo 401(k).

- If that $25,000 grew to $100,000 over a period of time, that $100,00 eventually becomes 100% tax-free money.

Now imagine putting in $25,000 per year for 10 years, which would total $250,000 in contributions. If you grew that $250,000 to over $1 million, that million dollars would be tax-free — that's the definition of wealth creation right there.

In 2021, the income limit to qualify for a Roth IRA is $140,000 of a modified adjusted income for single filers and $208,000 for joint filers. There is no income restriction on how much you can make annually per year income-wise when it comes to allowable contributions into a Roth Solo 401(k).

If you are a high-income earner, the Roth bucket is a great way to grow tax-free money.

For more valuable information that will last you a lifetime of earning, please sign up for my course "The Quest Way – How to Grow Your Money Tax Free" at

BluePrintRetirementCourse.com

You'll get the reader-exclusive price of $47, compared to the regular price of $297. Just visit the link above and register! It's that easy.

CHAPTER 5: COULD YOU USE CAPITAL TO GROW YOUR BUSINESS?

"An entrepreneur without financing is a musician without an instrument."
—Robert Rice

Before you read any further...

You should know that, if you aren't a business owner, you cannot take advantage of the Solo 401(k). Also, if you have W2 employees aside from you and your spouse, the Solo 401(k) was not designed for you. You have probably heard the line, "The rich get richer," and it is so true, because wealthy people understand wealth-building strategies that a lot of Americans don't comprehend or know about.

Currently, business owners in America receive tons of benefits. This is related to the laws that are put into place, and we all know that Congress has a big part in these laws.

Now, take a moment and think about who's sitting on Congress.

People in Congress probably have LLCs, S Corps, and side hustles. You know they have other businesses.

But why do Congress members invest their time and energy into side businesses?

They own and operate other companies because they can influence decisions that benefit themselves.

For example, Darrell Issa is the U.S. Representative for California's 50th congressional district. As of 2015, Issa was the richest member of congress. He made most of his fortune while leading Directed Electronics Inc, a manufacturer of vehicle antitheft devices that he created.

Another business owner in Congress is Texan Roger Williams. He owns several car dealerships and car washes in Fort Worth.

It's only natural that Congress has laws that benefit business owners, which in turn benefit them. So don't hate the players; hate the game.

A better option than wasting our time hating is to join them and benefit from these laws. The rules are there; we just have to be aware of them and know what we can and can't do as a result of them.

Knowing that there is nothing holding you back from leveraging these laws for yourself, why would you not join 'em?

They're doing it.

There's no difference between you and them.

You just have to choose to do it, too.

REINVENTING EVELYN

Evelyn was working a 9-5 job in the hair stylist world and hated it. She dreamed of leaving her job one day and starting an on-line business. So she did her research and learned she would need capital to make her transition happen. Evelyn didn't want to go into high-interest debt with the banks and knew it would be tough to get a loan from the bank, since banks are hesitant to lend money to new businesses with no track record. Evelyn wasn't a big fan of having all of her IRA in the stock market and she liked the idea of using some of that money to invest in her business. She approached her financial adviser about taking $15,000 from her account. He advised against it, saying she would be paying 30% in penalties and taxes. Evelyn left that conversation feeling discouraged.

Shortly thereafter, she learned about the Solo 401(k) and the ability to take money out of the account before retirement age penalty- and tax-free. As I mentioned, the Solo 401(k) has a loan feature where one can take out up to 50% of the account value or $50,000 (whichever number is less). The money has to be paid back within five years (minimum quarterly payments must be made) to avoid paying the 10% early withdrawal penalty and taxes. There is an interest rate on the loan, but the interest goes back to the Solo 401(k)—so Evelyn would be pay-ing herself. The interest rate is calculated at prime + 1% to 2%.

Evelyn converted her IRA into her new Solo 401(k). From there she took out $15,000 penalty- and tax-free and used that money to fund her business. That part played a big role in helping Evelyn eventually be able to quit her job and work full-time on her online business.

Evelyn got what she ultimately wanted: control, freedom, autonomy.

No one wants to be held captive, especially when it comes to our money. We worked for this money. And no one cares about our money more than we do. But if that's truly the case, why do we let ourselves get into the position where our money goes places that we can't control?

Why do we let ourselves get into situations where, if we try to control it and we access it, we get penalized?

This is why I advocate checking out a Solo 401(k).

It gives you ultimate control.

Keep in mind that the loan feature is not available on all 401(k) plans. There are certain 401(k) and Solo 401(k) plans that don't offer the loan feature. So do your research and recognize that when you take money out of your Solo 401k there is usually an opportunity cost. You must think about how to use that money wisely.

Here's more good news for you as a business owner.

MULTIPLE LOANS

If you want to take out more than one loan on the plan, you can. Just make sure that language in your plan documentation exists stating that you can have multiple loans on the 401(k). The IRS won't let you have multiple loans on a 401(k) if the combined loan balances exceed more than 50% of the account value or $50,000 (whichever number is less).

The loan feature through the Solo 401(k) is a nice option to use to fund your business. There is no credit check, income verification, or verification of funding based on how long your business has been around.

For more valuable information that will last you a lifetime of earning, please sign up for my course "The Quest Way – How to Grow Your Money Tax Free" at

BluePrintRetirementCourse.com

You'll get the reader-exclusive price of $47, compared to the regular price of $297. Just visit the link above and register! It's that easy.

CHAPTER 6: WHAT INVESTMENTS CAN BE HELD INSIDE A SOLO 401(K)?

"The Solo 401(k) gives you both sides of the menu when it comes to your investments."
— *Daniel Blue*

Since you're the business owner, you get to decide where you invest your money. What a powerful position to be in.

If you want to invest your Solo 401(k) in the stock market, you can do that. Some companies can set up a Solo 401(k) for you, allowing you to pick and choose different stocks, index funds, bonds, and ETFs (which stands for "exchange traded fund" and means that, instead of investing into one single stock, you can invest into a basket of different stocks). With a Solo 401(k), since you call the shots, you have a much bigger menu of investment options compared to the 401(k) you would normally participate in via your corporate job. Most 401(k)s that originate through the corporate world limit you to basic mutual funds.

SELF-DIRECTED SOLO 401(K)

Another type of investing style available through your Solo 401(k) is what is called a self-directed Solo 401(k). This Solo 401(k) allows you to invest your money outside the stock market.

Before I explain further, let me tell you a quick story about Mitt Romney and how he used a self-directed retirement account to make millions.

Most of us know a thing or two about taxes and what a 401(k) or IRA retirement account is. However, most of us do not understand what a self-directed retirement account is and how Mitt Romney used this particular account to reportedly make over $100 million. That's right, there was over $100 million inside his IRA.

But how exactly could Mitt Romney do this, and what in the heck is a self-directed retirement account?

To explain, and provide you with a little bit of context, I have to go back in time to when the IRA was born in 1974. That's when the "ERISA" (Employee Retirement Income Security Act) came into being, too. Since the banks and brokerage houses acted as custodians of the IRA, investment options were limited. This was due to the fact that the banks and brokerage houses focused solely on selling stocks, bonds, and mutual funds. These companies were unwilling to handle their IRA account holders' desire to invest in private businesses, precious metals, real estate, and other off-Wall Street investments.

By the early 1990s, IRAs had become more popular — in part because IRA account holders were looking for other ways to invest their IRA funds into other investments besides the stock market. Because of this demand, several trust companies with the administrative flexibility to hold alternative investments jumped into the IRA arena.

With these new companies in the market, it became possible for IRA investors to have their retirement assets in a "self-directed" position. Now investments into real estate, precious metals, and private companies were permitted within IRA accounts.

In short, a self-directed retirement account is a tax-savings vehicle that allows one to invest in alternative assets such as private equity, real estate, cryptocurrency, and precious metals. Mitt Romney took advantage of a self-directed SEP IRA and made private equity investments that catapulted his IRA account's value.

To clarify, you can have a self-directed Roth IRA, a self-directed traditional IRA, a self-directed SEP IRA like Mitt Romney had, or a self-directed Solo 401(k).

Self-directed Solo 401(k)s are very popular amongst real estate investors.

LEVERAGING REAL ESTATE

A friend of mine, Aaron, had a 401(k) from his previous employer. He wanted to use that money to invest in multi-family real estate. But the documentation in his 401(k) spelled out that he could only invest into stock-market based options.

That wasn't going to serve my friend Aaron's purpose. He wanted to invest in a flip and in some multi-family private lending deals. Since Aaron knew his current 401(k) plan wouldn't allow real estate investments, he converted his 401(k) from his old job into a Solo 401(k). Once the funds were inside his Solo 401(k), Aaron had the option to take out up to $50,000 as a loan to fund his flip and use the rest of his Solo 401(k) funds to invest in private lending.

The key to making alternative investments work inside a self-directed Solo 401(k) is finding a custodian that can administer these types of investments. Once you find a custodian, you can grow your alternative investments tax-deferred or tax-free within your Solo 401(k).

One thing to keep in mind as you learn more about your possibilities is that there are specific types of investments you can't make with a with a self-directed IRA or self-directed Solo 401(k). These are called prohibited transactions and they are set by the IRS.

Common prohibited transactions that can't be made include:

- Purchasing private equity shares in your business or that of any other disqualified person. (Here's an example of what I mean by "disqualified person": my customer "Bob" can't use his self-directed retirement account to invest into his son's business. Bob's son, in this scenario, is a disqualified person because of an IRS rule that states you can't use your retirement account to invest in someone/a business owned by a lineal descendant or yourself.)

- Purchasing real estate that you or other disqualified persons live in.

- Purchasing collectibles like art, gems, cars and antiques.

A disqualified person is considered a lineal descendant and can include relationships like parents and grandparents to you. A person providing services to the plan, such as a CPA or attorney, would also be considered a disqualified individual.

CHAPTER 7: DEBUNKING THE MYTH THAT YOU SHOULDN'T TOUCH YOUR RETIREMENT

"What you don't know can really hurt you . . .
and your bank account."
—Daniel Blue

We've covered that some people say you're *never* supposed touch your retirement account, and that you should *never* touch your IRA and 401(k).

Don't forget that the people insisting on this are people in the financial world. These are the people you trust to give you investment advice and to help you manage your different retirement vehicles. So, why would they say, "Don't touch your IRA dollars?" or "Don't touch your 401(k) dollars?"

THE ANSWER

It's simple.

You know by now that if you do tap into your retirement accounts at an early age, in some instances you will get nailed in penalties and taxes.

From that perspective, it makes sense. They *should* warn you about these potential issues.

It also makes sense for these investment professionals to advise their customers not to take money out of their retirement account if the customer is hell-bent on using that money for something stupid.

If we do make that decision to just blow our money, we are just draining our money away. That money could've sat in a 401(k) or an IRA; it could've been invested to make money. People who make rash decisions like these lose out on all the gains. Their money could've grown if they'd have left it in their account – if they had been patient and fought the desire for immediate gratification, versus taking out that money and using it somewhere that's not beneficial. Again, opportunity costs must be considered.

I agree with those two arguments that you should let your money sit. But the situation is more complicated than that.

FINANCIAL "ADVISORS"

What if I told you these "financial experts" have a darker reason for telling you not to touch your money?

A big reason why financial advisors advise, "Do not pull money out of your retirement account," is because they're making tons of fees off your money. You probably don't even know about many of these fees. I will get into these fees in greater detail later in this book, but suffice to say, there are many hidden fees buried amongst the fees you do see.

Never lose sight of the fact that you have the right to know *how you are spending your money and where your money is going — no matter the intentions of these "experts."*

MAKING MORE AND MORE MONEY OFF YOU

Some financial advisors make money off commissions that are generated in selling you certain investments. Secondarily, financial investors also make money off the assets under their management. The more money they have under management, the more money under their umbrella of business — which directly feeds into the increased fees they're making.

Knowing this, we can understand why it's not in your financial advisor's best interest to have you pulling your money out. It shrinks the amount of money under management — which lowers their pay. Of course, they are going to fight to keep that money — your money — right where it is! Wouldn't you fight like hell if someone was trying to take away your money? Ah, but it's not their money, is it? It's yours... however, financial advisors count your money as their money. How twisted is that?

I was talking to a friend who recently was in a situation where they needed to withdraw $50,000 from their IRA for bills. When I told them, "There is another way you can take money out of your retirement account, without having to lose 30% in penalties and taxes," they asked me, "Why has nobody told me about this before?" Again, this part had been left out of the explanation by their financial adviser. Educating their customers on how to access retirement money penalty and tax-free for the purposes of using the money outside the stock market goes against their financial business model.

I can't tell you how many times I've talked to business owners with money in an IRA and individual retirement accounts who have shared with me that they've withdrawn money from their IRA. The plot thickens when they get clobbered in penalties and taxes. If they have had their money in a Solo 401(k), they could have withdrawn that money as a loan and avoided having to pay those taxes and penalties.

As you continue reading, don't forget that no one cares about your money more than you do. I'm going to repeat that assertion in this book — it's that important.

Your financial advisor won't care more than you. The company that holds your money won't care more than you. Nobody cares more about your money than you, because you are the one who worked for it.

Your financial advisors could be making 0.5-1.5% per year off your money. Imagine how this adds up. It makes for a significant amount of money in aggregate. And don't worry, I also provide you with an example of these aggregated fees in a later chapter of this book, so you can see for yourself all the hidden fees that are designed to nickel-and-dime you to death.

To keep your money exactly where it is, financial advisors would rather scare you and say, "Move that money and you'll have to pay penalties and taxes." Or "Oh, you're going to get clobbered by the IRS." They use fear to keep your money in your retirement account.

If you take away nothing else from this book, take away this: this is your money that you've put in an IRA or 401(k). You earned it through hard work, long hours, and sacrificing more enjoyable parts of your lives — even time with loved ones. Keep that in mind when you hear that someone else wants to tell you how to control what you sacrificed and accumulated for your family and you. We should be able to control our money as best we can, and to use our money how we see fit.

YOU ACTUALLY CAN DO WHAT YOU WANT

Here's another upsetting fact: when you put money into your IRA, or you use your money to buy a mutual fund, your financial advisor makes a fat commission check off that transaction. Further, the financial company makes a percentage-based fee off your money.

It makes no sense that you can't use the money in your retirement account to buy real estate and purchase properties without paying penalties and taxes — until you remember that the big Wall Street firms don't make money this way. Besides, this misunderstanding doesn't apply to having an IRA with Fidelity. You can't use that money to buy real estate. So if you have money in an IRA and want to buy some property, go for it! (As long as the financial decision makes sense, of course.)

BIG FIRM LIES

I was talking to a customer recently who said they were going to withdraw $200,000 from their Fidelity IRA and invest it in real estate. The plan was to commit to paying a bunch of penalties and taxes — just so they could invest in real estate. They were all set to go, when they talked to their financial advisor, who informed them: "No, you can't use this money to buy real estate."

That's when the customer came to me to ask if this was accurate. I told the customer that there was a way to accomplish what they wanted to do. They could take their IRA and roll it over into a self-directed retirement account. They could then use the money in the self-directed retirement account to invest in real estate. The customer stared at me for a second and then asked, "Why didn't my financial advisor tell me this?"

You know the answer by now. It's not in their best interest. Again, it doesn't make them money, and it doesn't make their company money. They don't make a commission. They don't make fees.

As dishonest as this sounds, you have to understand that you are responsible for understanding what you have agreed to in your investments. These financial advisors are not under any obligation to volunteer that information to you. The understanding between the two of you is that you comprehend fully what you have agreed to and that you have signed your name to it.

Financial advisors don't need to disclose anything to you, and when pressed, they will even answer your questions to make a disbursement in a specific way: "You can't use this money to buy real estate." The financial advisor is correct in that the money in a specific vehicle cannot be used directly for that purpose. They are not correct in implying that there are no other ways to accomplish this aim. *But they don't have to do the brainstorming for you.* It is up to you to figure it out, to assemble more resources and learn about what you can do versus what you can't.

If you need to tap into your retirement account to buy real estate, invest in your business, or pay off high-interest debt, you can. There are ways to accomplish this. Understand, though, that doing this will get your financial advisor's undies in a wad. When you tell them what you are about to do, they will come at you with every argument and bring up every fear to get you to change your mind. As you sit there and listen to what they have to say, remember what their motivation is. It's not to take care of you. It is to continue earning off your investments.

Financial advisors use your money to invest in the stock market and make a bunch of fees off you. Let me ask you, *whose money is at risk? Theirs or yours?* I know you know the answer to this by now. It's yours. They're using your money and putting it at risk. If the stock market goes down, you lose money, but that doesn't matter to your financial advisor. Because guess who's still making fees? That's right! They are. The financial company that's holding your money will make money off you regardless of the state of the stock market.

So, the next time you hear, "Don't touch your retirement account," ask yourself a few questions.

- Who's telling me this?
- Why are they telling me this?
- Do they have a valid argument?

And finally...

- Does what they are saying have an agenda that benefits them?

For more valuable information that will last you a lifetime of earning, please sign up for my course "The Quest Way – How to Grow Your Money Tax Free" at

BluePrintRetirementCourse.com

You'll get the reader-exclusive price of $47, compared to the regular price of $297. Just visit the link above and register! It's that easy.

CHAPTER 8: ARE YOU LOSING MONEY FASTER THAN YOU ARE MAKING MONEY?

"Interest on debts grows without rain."
— *Yiddish Proverb*

I can't tell you how many times I've talked to somebody who has money in an IRA that is making them 7-9% a year while they also have credit card debt costing them 25% a year. Think about those numbers for a minute...

If one side of a coin is making you 7-9%, and the other side is costing you 25%, you are still losing money faster than you're making money.

When I talk to people with money in an IRA, and they've got credit card debt keeping them up at night, lowering their credit score, and stressing them out, I point out that they're upset because they know they're losing a lot of money. More accurately, they know they are losing money, but they don't know the available options to stop the bleeding. I always think that if *they just knew they could do something about it, they would sleep A LOT more soundly*!

Losing money faster than you're making money is obviously a huge problem.

SOLUTIONS TO STOP BLEEDING OUT

One solution is to use your Solo 401(k). Remember, the Solo 401(k) is a tool that allows you to pull money out of your retirement account *without* paying those ridiculous penalties and taxes.

One of our customers, Bob, had $50,000 in credit card debt with an interest rate of 20%. He was paying about $1,500 a month in payments towards the credit card debt. Bob also had an IRA worth $250,000 that was making him around 7% a year. To resolve his credit card debt, he converted his IRA into a Solo 401(k). From the Solo 401(k) he used the loan feature and took out $50,000 penalty- and tax-free. He then used those funds to pay off the credit card debt in one shot. This immediately brought up Bob's credit score, because removing all that credit card debt brought down his utilization rate. If you have a utilization rate of over 30-50%, your credit score will suffer. For example, if you have a credit card with a limit of $10,000 and a balance of $7,000, your credit score will not improve. Since Bob paid off so much of his credit card debt, his credit score shot through the roof. Another advantage to Bob paying off his $50,000 credit card debt in one shot was that there were no more $1,500 monthly payments to the banks.

Credit card debt is how so many people fall behind. They think they are making a difference in the principal when they make their payments, but the truth is that they are mostly chipping away at the interest. They're barely touching the principal.

When Bob was paying $1,500 to the banks each month, hundreds of dollars every month went toward the *interest* on the debt — which doesn't bring down the principal of the total debt. Lots of people think that if you owe $50,000 in credit card debt at 20% interest the annual interest rate would be calculated at 20% of $50,000, or $10,000 in interest each year. That's not true. Credit card companies charge you interest daily. And most people use their credit cards daily — which increases the principal and interest daily. They religiously make their payments but keep making charges on the card.

Credit card companies benefit from these types of arrangements, because 1) you might not ever be able to pay off what you owe, and 2) you will barely make any progress on the principal if the amount is high enough.

When Bob took the $50,000 from his Solo 401(k) to pay off his $50,000 credit card debt, he became his own bank.

Instead of making a payment to the credit card companies, he made a payment to his Solo 401(k) each month for five years. His monthly payment to his Solo 401(k) was calculated over a 5-year term at a fixed 5.25% interest rate. Remember, the Solo 401(k) loan interest goes back into his Solo 401(k) account.

Factoring in those numbers, his $50,000 Solo 401(k) loan produced a $949.00 monthly payment that Bob makes to his Solo 401(k). As long as Bob paid back his Solo 401(k) loan within five years, there were no penalties and taxes owed on the $50,000 he took out. More importantly, Bob replenished his retirement account so those funds could contribute to grow.

The 5.25% interest rate comes from the Solo 401k interest rate being what interest rate prime is set with an additional 1%-2%.

Bob wouldn't have been able to do this if he hadn't been a business owner. Because he's a business owner, he could tap into his retirement account to pay off his debt without paying the penalties and taxes by using the Solo 401(k).

When you contrast these two situations, it's a pretty simple decision.

1. Be at the bank's mercy and chip away at the credit card each month over the years as the interest stacks up.

2. Be your own bank and pay yourself back the money plus interest.

Earlier we talked about how Bob's credit score went up because he paid off his credit card debt. I want to stress the importance of having a good credit score. Life is a lot easier with a better credit score. If you get a car loan, your interest rate is lower, which saves you tons of money.

Maybe you want to buy a house or refinance your existing mortgage. If you purchase a house, a $250,000 loan over 30 years at 5% will cost you $233,139.46 in interest. On the other hand, if you take a $250,000 loan over 30 years at 3%, it will cost you $129,443.63 in interest. If you have an excellent credit score, there is a much better chance you can lock in a low interest rate on your mortgage.

Good credit puts more money in your pocket.

One thing to consider when taking money out as a loan from your Solo 401(k) is the opportunity cost. If you left your funds inside your retirement account, that money could grow over time. You already know the options if you take it out. So just make sure that you weigh out the pros and cons.

Will the funds taken from your Solo 401(k) loan be used to put more money in your pocket in comparison to what the funds would be doing inside your retirement account if you don't touch the money?

If you factor in situations like the one I talked about in this chapter, such as saving thousands of dollars from credit card interest rates and possibly $100,000+ in savings on a mortgage loan, the Solo 401(k) loan feature is definitely an option worth considering.

For more valuable information that will last you a lifetime of earning, please sign up for my course "The Quest Way – How to Grow Your Money Tax Free" at

BluePrintRetirementCourse.com

You'll get the reader-exclusive price of $47, compared to the regular price of $297. Just visit the link above and register! It's that easy.

CHAPTER 9: WALL STREET'S
DIRTY LITTLE SECRET...

"Follow the money."
—1976 docudrama film All the President's Men

WARREN BUFFET SAYS...

"When trillions of dollars are managed by Wall Streeters charging high fees, it will usually be the manager who reaps outsized profits, not the customers."

I've asked people over the years who have an IRA or a 401(k) how much they're paying in fees for their account. Their reply is usually, "I'm not paying any fees."

I usually think, *I didn't know the company that holds your IRA or 401(k) is a nonprofit. That's interesting.*

What's also interesting concerns someone we've all heard of: Warren Buffett. He's one of the most successful financial gurus and investors.

In the last century, Warren Buffett made a bet with a really, really big hedge fund guy. A hedge fund is an alternative investment fund that aims to beat the performance of the overall stock market. The bet went something like this:[5]

---

[5] Wiles, Russ. "Warren Buffett Made a 10-Year Bet on His Market Strategy. Here's How He Won." USA Today. Gannett Satellite Information Network,

Buffett bet that the investment he picked over a 10-year period of time would do better over that same 10-year period than the hedge fund guy's investment pick. Buffett chose a basic fund that followed the S&P 500. He simply invested in the biggest companies in America based on their performance.

The other guy's investment was a fancy hedge fund. Warren Buffet bet a pretty large sum of money that his pick would win, and the loser of the bet had to pay a large sum of money to a charity. Buffett was super, super confident that his bet would beat the hedge fund guy. His bet wasn't as sexy as the other guy's; still, he knew he would win over a 10-year period of time, because his investment had minimal fees.

The investment that the hedge fund guy picked had a decent amount of fees. Buffett said to the guy who he bet against, "The investment that you're picking has a lot of fees, and those fees are going to eat at the returns year after year."

Buffet ended up winning the bet. As he predicted, his pick had a better rate of return over a 10-year period of time than the hedge fund guy's. A lot of that had to do with the lower fees associated with Buffet's pick.

March 7, 2018.
https://www.usatoday.com/story/money/markets/2018/03/07/warren-buffett-made-10-year-bet-his-market-strategy-heres-how-he-won/402823002/.

WE CAN LEARN FROM WARREN BUFFET'S PICK...

Seven out of ten people don't know how much they are paying in fees inside their 401(k) accounts.[6] Not knowing the fees inside a retirement account can eat at the total sum of money and impact your lifestyle as you get older.

Let's examine a $50,000 investment that returns 6% per year and has a total annual fee of 2.25% held for 30 years. After 30 years, the value totals $145,093.83. A fund with the same amount invested and the same annual returns but a yearly fee of 0.45% would total $250,832.55 after 30 years. That a difference of over $100,000 dollars!

So why don't we care about the fees that build up and erode our wealth? It's not so much a question of not caring, it's more a lack of knowledge.

That's just how Wall Street has it set up — hiding most of the fees, so that even when you go on the hunt for them in your statements, they aren't easy to find.

THE 411 ON FEES

If you have money in an IRA, 401(k) or other non-retirement investment account, you are most likely paying a couple of fees.

---

[6] Investor Pulse Survey. Ameritrade, January 2018.
https://s1.q4cdn.com/959385532/files/doc_downloads/research/FY2018/Investor-Sentiment-Infographic-401k-fees.pdf.

The first type of fee that you might be paying is some type of plan fee or administrative fee. This will be a nominal fee and add up to maybe $50 a year or a couple of hundred dollars a year. This is a popular arrangement if you have a 401(k).

The other kind of fee that you're going to pay is a fee to your financial adviser. How do you know if you're paying this particular fee? The easiest way to determine this is to ask yourself: *do I pick the investments inside my account, or does someone else pick the investments inside my account?*

If you're the one who picks where you invest your money, deciding you want to put X amount in Apple stock, X amount in a particular index fund, and X amount on Netflix stock, — then most likely *you're not* paying the managed fee.

If you're pretty hands-off on your portfolio – meaning you're not picking and choosing where to invest your money – that means somebody else is. And they're not doing it for free. This means you *will* pay a managed fee. Sometimes the managed fee is called a wrapped fee.

If someone is watching over your account and picking and choosing where your money goes, they might charge you more than just the managed fee. There are potentially two types of ways they can charge you.

First, they might charge you a percentage cut based off the money they're overseeing and managing for you. For example, if you have $100,000 with them in your IRA, and a 0.5% managed fee, then you can tabulate that you're paying $500 a year to have your advisor manage your account. As we have discussed, the percentages of these fees can vary. They may be 1% per year, they may be 1.5% per year.

Sometimes this percentage-based fee you pay to your financial adviser is in plain sight on your quarterly or monthly statement. Other times it's not listed on the statement — but you should know about it, and you should also know what you are paying.

If your financial adviser isn't charging you an annual percentage-based fee for your account to manage your funds, that means they are making money off your account through commissions produced by the mutual funds inside your account.

For example, each time your advisor purchases a mutual fund that is classified as a Class A mutual fund, it produces an upfront commission paid to the financial company and your advisor. That sales commission could anywhere from 2-5.75% paid upfront.

But what's the math?

If you used $100,000 to buy a mutual fund, a 5% percent (or $5,000) fee was charged to you.

That mutual fund you invested in is also most likely going to kick off dividends. Dividends are the income this investment is producing.

Dividends are typically paid to you each quarter. It's income the mutual fund generates that flows back into your account. A lot of times that same money is used to purchase more Class A mutual funds. It's a case of lather, rinse and repeat as your money is used again to repurchase the same Class A mutual fund.

This cycle produces another commission to your financial advisor, and the financial company. Yep, that's another 5% for them!

To recap: your financial advisor and financial company make money off you *upfront*, whether your investment makes money or not. No matter if that mutual fund goes up or down, they still make their commission. So if you see a Class A mutual fund, you need to at least understand what you are paying upfront. *Are you paying 3% upfront? Are you paying 5% upfront?*

These fees can mean a difference of thousands of dollars.

FEES BREAKDOWN

1. You've got admin fees.

2. You've got financial advisor fees.

3. You've got internal fees — annual fees for the actual investments themselves.

Without drilling down into it, those fees are hard to read. How will you know if you're paying fees for the investments themselves?

We can start uncovering this information by determining what kind of investments you have. If you're investing your money into stocks, like Apple and Amazon, there won't be any internal investment fees. No one, human or robot, is managing your money amongst a basket of companies.

But what if you're investing money into mutual funds, index funds, or ETFs? These are really popular nowadays. These investments require fees to be assessed, because people are actually managing your money. If your money is in mutual funds, and you pay Carl, your financial advisor, 1% per year to oversee your mutual funds, is he really "managing" your funds, though? No, he is not. Although he will still get paid!

Another party is managing a lot of your money, and you don't even know who it is.

Let me makes this a whole lot clearer to you.

CARL, THE ADVISOR

If you have $100,000 with your advisor Carl in an IRA and you bought a couple of mutual funds, the mutual fund is run not by Carl, but by fund managers. Most likely, these fund managers are managing billions of dollars. They also have a team. They have a staff, researchers, and an overheard they need to pay. These fund managers are essentially a business.

They have expenses, and they pass along these expenses to the investors — people who put money into their mutual funds. This fee is called an expense ratio. An expense ratio is a fee that is calculated annually. The expense ratio could be anywhere from .25-1.50%

If you have $100,000 in this mutual fund and your expense ratio is 1% per year, that is $1,000 a year, give or take, that you're paying for — to have this mutual fund.

A lot of these fees that we're discussing are buried in your statements. Sometimes they're not even evident in the IRA or 401(k)'s quarterly or monthly statement that you get. So it's not in the best interest of these financial companies to be forthcoming with you.

Could you imagine rolling over your 401(k) from the job that you just left into an IRA and then being told upfront that your financial advisor is going to charge you 1% per year to "manage your money"? But it gets better: he's going to put you in some mutual funds that are going to charge you another 1% per year for those expense ratios for the mutual funds.

Suddenly, you're paying 2% a year. If you have $200,000 in investments, 2% a year equals $4,000 a year in fees. Do the calculations, and that's $20,000 in fees over five years that you have to pay! Do you think if your financial advisor told you the truth about the fees they are going to charge you upfront that you would make that decision to stay with them, to invest as you wanted to initially? Maybe you would think about it a little bit more before you made the move.

HOW TO FIND THE INFORMATION YOU NEED

The best part of this bad news is: this information is accessible. We live in a day and age where technology is right at our fingertips. If you have an IRA or a 401(k), you get a statement. That's all you need to get to the bottom of what you are being charged. I encourage you to look at the "holdings" page of your statement. It will give you the breakdown you need. Using our example of $100,000 again, you'll see perhaps $25,000 on a mutual fund, $25,000 on a stock, etc. Start at the top and move your way down the statement.

Under the name of the mutual fund, you might see what's called a ticker symbol. The ticker symbol is made up of 3-5 unique letters that are used only in that arrangement for that mutual fund. If "ABC" mutual fund is on your statement, next to it you might see a specific ticker symbol, like ABALX. Great! ABALX is the ticker symbol for American Funds American Balanced Fund Class A.

Next, Google that ticker symbol. When you do, it will give you information about that investment. You can also visit a website like morningstar.com or Google Finance. If your money is with Fidelity or another financial company, go to that website and look up that mutual fund.

This is public information, so you can just Google the mutual fund and when a few links pull up, click on one of them. On that site, you'll see the expense ratio. You can ascertain when you look at this info, for instance, "Okay, I'm paying 1%

a year for this mutual fund. And I'm paying 0.5% a year for this mutual fund." At the same time, you can find out if the mutual fund is costing you a sales commission. You want to know if you are paying an upfront load to the financial company for this mutual fund.

Taking time once a year to go through your statement is a smart exercise. I relate doing this to lifting up the hood of your car. You want to make sure everything looks and smells good, because never forget...this is your money.

Nobody cares about your money more than you do.

Not your financial advisor.

Not the financial company who holds your money.

You made that money.

You earned that money, not them.

So naturally you're going to care about it more than they do.

Take time and look at your money. If you have money in an IRA or 401(k), I know you will feel a lot better just knowing how much you're paying per year in fees. You also need to know how much your money is making you. You didn't set all that money aside to make minimal returns. If you didn't care about the return, you would have left it in your bank account. And the banks are giving you roughly 0.5% a year if you're lucky? CDs are paying next to nothing. Money in your savings is not working for you.

This is why you have elected to put it in a retirement account. You want it to grow. So understand how every piece of your money is allocated. *If you're making 8% per year, but you're paying 2% per year in fees, you're only making 6% a year.* The difference between making 2% more and paying 2% more is a big one — especially over five, ten, fifteen, and twenty years.

Know your money. Know your fees. Know how much you're paying. Know how much you're making.

To quote the great Albert Einstein, "Those who understand interest, earn it, those who don't, pay it."

FEES AFFECT EVERYONE AT EVERY AGE

My Grandma has an IRA. She didn't think she was paying any fees for her account. I sat down with her, grabbed her statement, and we dove into her holdings. After an extensive dissection of her accounts, we saw that her statement didn't show any fees, and deeper research to see if there were any hidden fees didn't reveal any. But then we went to her positions and saw that she had some mutual funds, so we grabbed those ticker symbols and Googled them.

On her Class A mutual funds, she was paying about 5% in commissions to her financial advisor and the financial company (a fee triggered every time money is used to purchase a Class A mutual fund). Her expense ratio was about 1% per year. But her statement didn't tell her this. It wasn't there in front of her, so she had no idea what she was really paying. It took some digging. It took lifting the hood of the car and assessing what was going on there. It took asking some questions and finding the answers.

In closing, make sure you have a B.L.U.E. print for your finances. Make sure you know what's going on. It's hard to take action without one, and it's hard to make decisions without the information in front of you. Looking at your statements reveals the direction of where your money is going.

As of 2021, taxes are changing. Inflation is changing. Cryptocurrency is being talked about left and right. With all these changes, it's important to consider that what has worked for people decades ago may not work the same way in this new digital age. You need to be informed, because these changes will impact your finances.

For more valuable information that will last you a lifetime of earning, please sign up for my course "The Quest Way – How to Grow Your Money Tax Free" at

BluePrintRetirementCourse.com

You'll get the reader-exclusive price of $47, compared to the regular price of $297. Just visit the link above and register! It's that easy.

CHAPTER 10: OLD-SCHOOL VERSUS NEW-SCHOOL

"What's worked in the past doesn't
mean it's going to work today."
—*Daniel Blue*

As you might have guessed from the title of this chapter, there are two types of ways you can have your retirement dollars set up. One is the old-school way, the other is the new-school way.

OLD-SCHOOL

Old-school means you have your money with a Wall Street company, and you only have investments in your account tied to the stock market — such as stocks and mutual funds. If this is the case, you will also pay a lot of the fees I discussed in the earlier chapters of this book. You will stick with basic accounts like an IRA or a 401(k) through your job. That's my definition of how an old-school retirement account is set up.

NEW-SCHOOL

The 2021 version of having your retirement dollars set up is taking advantage of the Solo 401(k), where you can access your retirement dollars penalty- and tax-free. Where you can invest your money outside the stock market and take advantage of tax-free growth using the Roth component of the Solo 401(k).

The problem with the old school way is that the companies behind the old school set up don't want your money in a self-directed retirement account. Your financial advisor likely won't know what a Solo 401k or a self-directed retirement account are. Self-directed retirement accounts have been around for decades. People don't know about them because, again, they're not talked about. It's not in the best interest of these big financial companies to talk about self-directed retirement accounts. Why would they teach you about a specific retirement account that allows you to take money from your account penalty and tax-free and invest it into assets that are not tied to Wall Street? They wouldn't, because that doesn't make them money. As the old saying goes, "Follow the money."

What's interesting to note is that when financial advisors and companies that operate in the traditional stock market arena *do* talk about self-directed retirement accounts, they don't talk about them in a positive manner. They usually bring up all of the negative consequences of having these kinds of accounts.

Granted, some areas in the self-directed retirement world have come under scrutiny.

Let's analyze those statements.

NEGATIVE POSSIBILITIES

Financial advisors say negative things about self-directed accounts like, "Be careful with them. You're going to get scammed. The IRS is going to audit you."

Sure.

The IRS may take an extra look and be a little more cautious when they see that someone has a self-directed retirement account because unfortunately some knuckleheads out there have used their self-directed retirement money to go on vacation. They have used that money to buy a property and live in it. Those are called prohibited transactions, which will cost you money in the form of taxes and penalties.

TIRED BOB

Bob wants to buy real estate and bury this argument about what he can do with his money once and for all. Bob has money in an IRA and he's in a bunch mutual funds. Now he's getting tired of the market, tired of fees, tired of not being in control of his money.

Bob likes real estate.

He wants to use the money in his retirement account to purchase real estate. Instead of withdrawing all the money from his IRA and paying penalties in taxes and then using that money to buy real estate, Bob can roll over his $250,000 from his IRA into his self-directed 401(k) account and use *that* $250,000 to buy a property.

But Bob can't live in it, nor can Bob do any of the work around the house (such as rehabbing it) himself. He has to hire a third-party contractor. Also, any rental payments that come from the property have to flow back into Bob's self-directed 401(k).

If Bob finds a property he can purchase for $200,000, he will use the money inside his self-directed 401(k) to purchase that property outright. *This means his 401(k) owns this property.* Now he rents the property out. This renter makes the rental payment every month and every month that rental payment goes right back into Bob's 401(k). Bob is essentially getting a monthly dividend payment. Every month, Bob is seeing money deposited into his 401(k) from the rental payment. We all know over time (within a degree of accuracy) that real estate's going to appreciate. Predictably (and if the market cooperates), Bob's property that he bought for $200,000 will most likely go up in value over a period of time.

This is an important point, so keep reading!

At some point, Bob can choose to sell this property.

Guess where that money goes from the sale of his property?

Yep. Right back into his 401(k). Boom! A bonus is that Bob is not taxed on any profit from the sale. Bob can move onto the next item on his agenda.

It is important to keep in mind that, if Bob's self-directed 401(k) owns a rental property, he cannot write off any property depreciation.

Again, if you have a 401(k) or an IRA with a Wall Street-based company, you can't invest in a truly self-directed manner. Remember, these strategies don't make Wall Street any money, so why wouldn't they discourage you from setting up a self-directed retirement account?

It all comes down to money.

These financial companies are making percentage points off you and profiting to the tune of approximately 1% per year for managing your money.

Here's some basic math. If they're managing $100M and making 1%, that's $1M per year.

If they're managing $500M, that's $5M. That's a lot of money.

It all adds up.

The more money you take out from under the financial advisors and financial company's umbrella, the more the fee goes down. When this happens, that affects the lifestyle of the people who are paid to manage YOUR MONEY. Suddenly you're talking about *their* boats and houses and cars and kids' educations. You're talking *their* vacations and second homes, etc. *You* are directly affecting the quality of *their* life every day.

This is why your financial advisor and your financial company are not going to give up that information voluntarily and sometimes, (as wrong as this is), even willingly.

For more valuable information that will last you a lifetime of earning, please sign up for my course "The Quest Way – How to Grow Your Money Tax Free" at

BluePrintRetirementCourse.com

You'll get the reader-exclusive price of $47, compared to the regular price of $297. Just visit the link above and register! It's that easy.

CHAPTER 11: ASK MORE
AND BETTER QUESTIONS

"It is not the answer that enlightens but the question."
—*Eugene Ionesco*

I think we can agree that in school we should be taught more about how credit scores work, how LLCs work, how mortgages work, how credit card interest works, the different ways to invest your money, and how retirement accounts work.

That's real life.

How many times have you encountered a financial challenge only to think *geez, I wish I had learned this in school*!?

FOLLOW THE GREEN ARROW

We have been conditioned to think a certain way. To follow the green arrow. You remember Fidelity, the financial service company that had a popular TV commercial where people followed the green arrow? The commercial instructed the actors to simply, "Follow the green arrow, and we'll show you the way."

I would see that commercial and think, *man, that's what they want us to do.* They want us to be like sheep and follow along. Don't ask questions. Just give us your money. We'll talk to you maybe once a year, when it's time to reinvest your money. That's what that green arrow meant to me.

A BETTER WAY

In the financial advising industry, there should be more dialogue; there should be more listening and more question-asking. I'm not saying all financial professionals do their customers wrong. But a lot of financial professionals exist only to serve themselves. They don't go into business to solve problems, ask questions, and find solutions for people.

Self-directed retirement accounts serve a place in this country. I don't think it's a good idea to have all your money in a self-directed retirement account, just like I don't think it's a good idea to have all your money in a Wall Street-based retirement account. Diversification exists for a reason. How your money is invested should also depend on your age, goals, liquidity needs and risk tolerance.

Again, a very small percentage of people even know what a self-directed retirement account is, let alone have one. It's my mission to bring this information to the public so they know more about it. Because the more they know, the better questions they can ask.

Better questions lead to better answers
which lead to better decisions.
Better decisions lead to better outcomes.

My goal isn't to get you to sign up for a self-directed retirement account. I simply want you to have the information about the different options available to you so you can make the best decision that suits your life.

WHAT DO I ASK?

A big problem people have is not knowing which questions to ask. The goal of this book is to provide you with enough information to ask more questions, to do more due diligence, to conduct more research, to allow you the freedom to think and greater peace of mind. You will feel better knowing your money is doing what you want it to do — whatever that might be.

We're blessed to live in the USA, where we have a bunch of freedom. We have a lot of control over our lives.

We should have freedom and control when it comes to our money. Especially our retirement accounts.

Self-directed retirement accounts give people more control than old-school Wall Street-based retirement accounts.

I hope reading this book has revealed to you valuable information that you can use to improve your life financially.

Your hard-earned money *can* work for you. You just have to know how to utilize it properly.

We've solved one half of that equation.

It's time for you to figure out the other half.

ACKNOWLEDGMENTS

I want to thank the women in my life for being lighthouses and very special people.

My mom, wife, and daughter push me to be a better person today than I was yesterday.

I also want to thank my employees at Quest Education. This book wouldn't have been possible without the combined decades of experience my staff has in the financial arena.

Last, but not least, I want to thank my entrepreneur friends who live all over the country who help me see what's possible.

You know who you are.

GLOSSARY

401(k) Loan Feature

In most cases, one can borrow up to 50% of the 401(k) account value or $50,000 (whichever number is less). The loan has a 5-year term and an interest rate of prime + 1%-2%. Principal and interest payments go back into the 401(k). No taxable event is trigged on the money taken out as long as the loan does not go into default.

Catch-Up Contributions

A catch-up contribution is a type of retirement savings contribution that allows people aged 50 or older to make additional contributions to 401(k) accounts and individual retirement accounts (IRAs). When a catch-up contribution is made, the total contribution will be larger than the standard contribution limit. (Source: Investopedia)

Disqualified Person

Disqualified persons include the IRA owner's fiduciary and members of his or her family (spouse, ancestor, lineal descendant, and any spouse of a lineal descendant). (Source: IRS.gov)

ETF

The term stock exchange-traded fund (ETF) refers to a security that tracks a particular set of equities. These ETFs trade on exchanges the same way normal stocks do and track equities just like an index. They can track stocks in a single industry or an entire index of equities. Investors who purchase shares of stock exchange ETF can gain exposure to a basket of equities and limited company-specific risk associated with single stocks, providing them with a cost-effective way to diversify their portfolios. (Source: Investopedia)

Holdings

Holdings are the contents of an investment portfolio held by an individual or an entity, such as a mutual fund or a pension fund. Portfolio holdings may encompass a wide range of investment products, including stocks, bonds, mutual funds, options, futures, and exchange traded funds (ETFs). (Source: Investopedia)

Index Funds

An index fund is a type of mutual fund or exchange-traded fund (ETF) with a portfolio constructed to match or track the components of a financial market index, such as the Standard & Poor's 500 Index (S&P 500). An index mutual fund is said to provide broad market exposure, low operating expenses, and low portfolio turnover. These funds follow their benchmark index regardless of the state of the markets. (Source: Investopedia)

Mutual Fund

A mutual fund is a type of financial vehicle made up of a pool of money collected from many investors to invest in securities like stocks, bonds, money market instruments, and other assets. (Source: Investopedia)

Prohibited Transaction

A prohibited transaction is a transaction between a plan and a disqualified person that is prohibited by law. (Source: IRS.gov)

Roth Contribution

A special retirement account where you pay taxes on money going into your account, and then all future withdrawals are tax-free. Roth IRAs are best when you think your taxes will be higher in retirement than they are right now. You can't contribute to a Roth IRA if you make too much money.
(Source: Investopedia)

Self-Directed Retirement Account

A *self-directed* retirement account is an account held by a custodian that allows investment in a broader set of assets than is permitted by most retirement account custodians. (Source: SEC)

SEP IRA

A retirement savings plan established by employers—including self-employed people—for the benefit of their employees and themselves. Employers may make tax-deductible contributions on behalf of eligible employees to their SEP IRAs. (Source: Investopedia)

SIMPLE IRA

A retirement savings plan that most small businesses with 100 or fewer employees can use. "SIMPLE" stands for "Savings Incentive Match Plan for Employees," and "IRA" stands for "Individual Retirement Account." Employers can choose to make a non-elective contribution of 2% of the employee's salary or a dollar-for-dollar matching contribution of the employee's contributions to the plan up to 3% of their salary. (Source: Investopedia)

Solo 401(k)

A solo 401(k) is an individual 401(k) designed for a business owner with no employees. (Source: Nerd Wallet)

Stock

A stock (also known as equity) is a security that represents the ownership of a fraction of a corporation. This entitles the owner of the stock to a proportion of the corporation's assets and profits equal to how much stock they own. Units of stock are called "shares." (Source: Investopedia)

Traditional (Pre-Tax) Contribution

Any contribution made to a designated pension plan, retirement account, or another tax-deferred investment vehicle for which the contribution is made before federal and municipal taxes are deducted. (Source: Investopedia)

Utilization Rate

Credit utilization refers to the amount of credit you have used compared with how much credit you have been extended by a lender. It also refers to a ratio that lenders use to determine your creditworthiness and is a factor that is used to determine your credit score. (Source: BankRate)

ABOUT THE AUTHOR

Daniel is a member of the Forbes Finance Council and is the owner of Quest Education. His company helps entrepreneurs access their retirement accounts in a penalty and tax-free way before retirement age. With over ten years of educating small business owners, Daniel has a knack for helping individuals get creative with their finances, leading to life-changing results.

DISCLAIMER

This Book provides general educational information on various topics, which should not be construed as professional, financial, real-estate, career, tax or legal advice. The information set forth in this Book is provided solely for informational purposes on an "as is" basis at your sole risk. The information is not meant to be, and should not be construed as advice or used for investment purposes. The author does not provide tax, investment or financial services and advice and are the author's personal opinions only.

The author makes no guarantees as to the accurateness, quality, or completeness of the information and the author shall not be responsible or liable for any errors, omissions, or inaccuracies in the information or for any reader's reliance on the information.

You are solely responsible for verifying the information as being appropriate for your personal use, including without limitation, seeking the advice of a qualified professional regarding any specific financial, investment, legal, tax, real-estate or other questions you may have.

The author is neither endorsed by or affiliated with any financial regulatory authority, agency, or association nor is the author a securities broker/dealer or an investment advisor.

The material contained in this Book is intended only for general information purposes and is not intended to be advice on any particular matter. Information provided in Book might not be suitable for all investors. Information is being presented without consideration of the investment objectives, risk tolerance or financial circumstances of any specific investor.

You are responsible for your own investment decisions. The author urges you to seek professional advice before acting on the basis of any information contained in the Book. Any recommendations made by the author is based on his personal experiences, but it is still your responsibility to conduct your own due diligence to ensure you have obtained complete accurate information about such product, services, coaches and consultants.

The Book has been prepared on the basis of latest prevailing provisions of different laws, rules and regulations made therein with the possible interpretation as per the author's understating of such laws, rules and regulations. The author is in no way responsible or liable for any financial or other losses of any kind arising on account of any action taken pursuant to the results or interpretation of this Book.

Reproduction, redistribution, use and transmission of any information contained in the Book are strictly prohibited.

Every effort has been made to avoid errors or omission. In spite of this, errors of omissions may occur. Although the author strives to provide accurate general information, the information presented here is not a substitute for any kind of professional advice, and you should not rely solely on this information. Always consult a professional in the area for your particular needs and circumstances prior to making any professional, legal, career, professional and financial or tax related decisions.

Made in the USA
Las Vegas, NV
29 August 2021

29235994R00059